JAZZICAL PIANO

Classical Favorites Played in Jazz Style

by
J. Douglas Esmond

Design & Typography by Roy "Rick" Dains

ISBN: 978-1-57424-319-2

Copyright ©2015 CENTERSTREAM Publishing, LLC
P. O. Box 17878 - Anaheim Hills, CA 92817
email: centerstream@aol.com • **web:** centerstream-usa.com

From the Author

I created this book with the thought that I could take the timeless melodies and pieces that we are so familiar with from the great composers of the Classical, Romantic and Baroque periods and give them a fresh start. Even though I don't consider myself a jazz musician as many of us who mostly live in the classical or other worlds of music, I love and appreciate Jazz. In the spirit of this musical form, I wanted to create pieces which had, in addition to an offbeat rhythmic structure and a more elaborate and lush harmonic scheme, the sense of freedom that Jazz offers. And I encourage all who play these pieces to embellish further, just as any improviser would, once the tune was introduced in its purest form. With each tune I chose different ways (i.e.; change of time signature, etc.) to subtly (and not so subtly!) change details while retaining the wonderful character of the originals. So whether you're a Classical music buff or a Jazz enthusiast you will find something to love!

About the Author

James Douglas Esmond was born April 18th, 1975. His first instrument, started at an early age, was the piano. He received his Bachelor's of Music Theory and Classical Guitar performance from Ithaca College, Ithaca, N.Y. Upon graduating he became involved in church music. He has held positions in various churches, as a guitarist,

organist, singer and conductor. In addition to his church work, he also teaches Guitar and Piano at Blue Sky Studios in Delmar, N.Y., and writes and arranges compositions in various genres and styles. He currently serves as the Organist/Music Coordinator at Newtonville United Methodist Church in Loudonville, N.Y. and He resides in Albany N.Y. with his wife Meighan and daughter, Evelyn. You can visit him on the web at : **jdesmondmusic.com.**

Table of Contents

Cool Dreams

(Brahm's Lullaby)

Johannes Brahms
arr. by J.Douglas Esmond

Pedal harmonically throughout

Joyful Jaunt

(based on "Ode to Joy")

L.V.Beethoven
arr. by J.Douglas Esmond

Happily

♩=**110-120**

Joyful Jaunt - *continued*

The intense musical genius,
Ludwig Van Beethoven

The Missing Variation

(based on 12 variations on "Ah, Vous Diraj-je Maman,"
otherwise known as "Twinkle, Twinkle, Little Star.")

W.A. Mozart,
arr. by J. Douglas Esmond

Heavy swing
♩=66

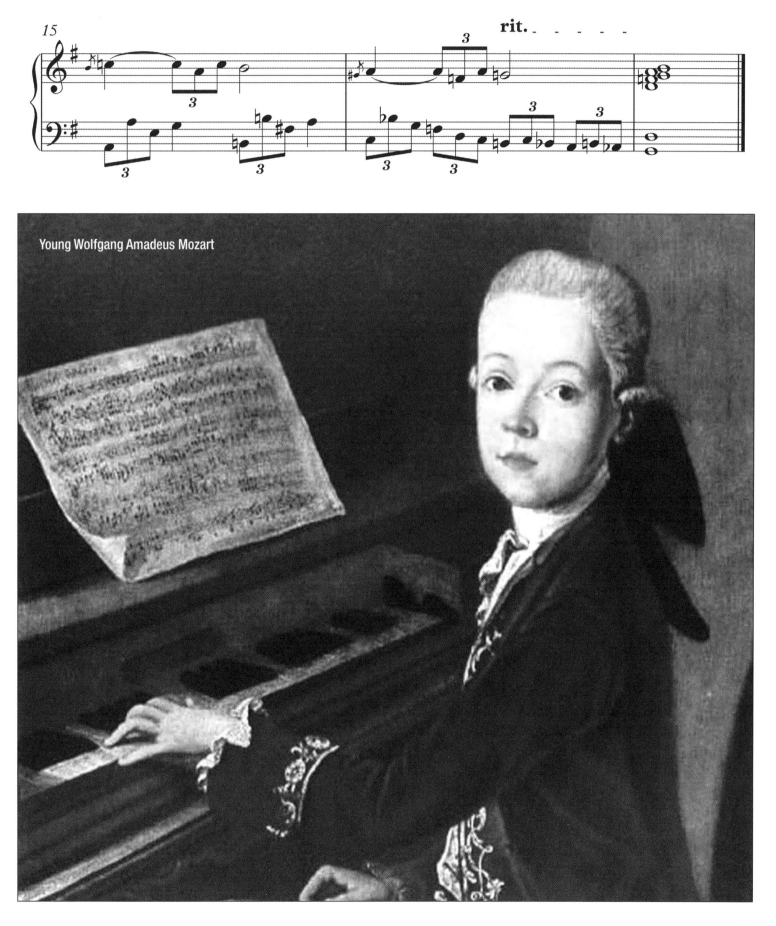

Young Wolfgang Amadeus Mozart

For Evelyn

(based on "Fur Elise")

L.V.Beethoven
arr. by J.Douglas Esmond

For Evelyn - *continued*

A Night on the Town

(based on "Eine Kleine Nachtmusic")

W.A.Mozart
arr. by J.Douglas Esmond

Merrily

♩=116

Piano

A Night on the Town - *continued*

Art Tatum
Early Master of Jazz Piano

The Queen of Shee-Bop

(based on "Arrival of the Queen of Sheba")

G.F.Handel
arr. by J.Douglas.Esmond

The Queen of Shee-Bop - *continued*

Jazzy Joys

(based on "Jesu, Joy of Man's Desiring")

J.S.Bach
arr. by J.Douglas Esmond

With a sacred swing

♩=92

Piano

Jazzy Joys - *continued*

It's a "New," New World

(based on a theme from the 2nd Movement of the "9th Symphony")

Antoine Dvorak
arr. by J.Douglas Esmond

Reverently and sweetly

♩=**110-120**

Piano

Bocc's Bop

(based on "Minuet for String Quintet, Op.11, No. 5")

Luigi Boccherini
arr. by J.Douglas Esmond

L.H. detached

Pedal harmonically ---

Bocc's Bop - *continued*

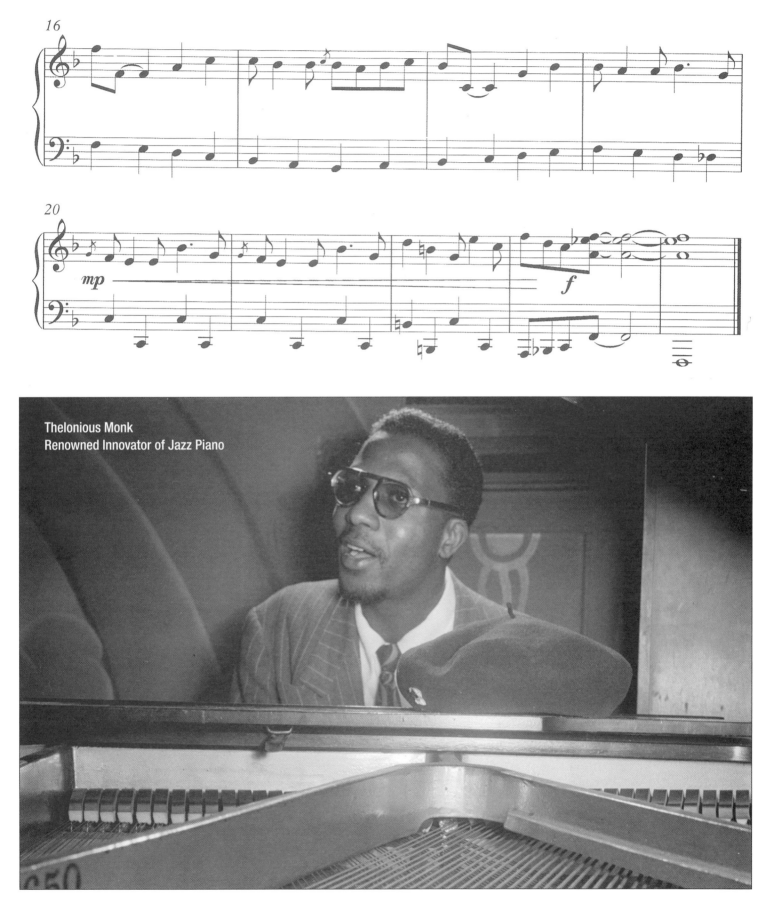

Thelonious Monk
Renowned Innovator of Jazz Piano

Cool Shuffle

(based on "Andante from Holberg Suite")

Edvard Grieg
arr. by J.Douglas Esmond

Introspectively

♩=**80**

Piano

Pedal harmonically

22

Cool Shuffle - *continued*

Canon in Blue

(based on "Canon in D")

Johann Pachelbel
arr. by J.Douglas Esmond

Canon in Blue - *continued*

Jazzy G March

(based on "Minuet in G")

J.S.Bach
arr. by J.Douglas Esmond

Racous, edgy

♩=**102**

Piano

Jazzy G March - *continued*